the
nature
of
boundaries

A little book of akashic wisdom—written by Laura Coe;
Guided by the Akashic Records.

LAURA COE

ISBN: 978-1-7373699-1-2 | Printed in the United States of America

Dedication

Thankfully, the universe spoke, and I listened.

Then love spoke, and I kept listening.

Introduction

This is a story about love. This is a story about a return to love. A return to self-love and a return to the joy that lay dormant, in need of resurrection. This is my story, told in part by me and in part by the energy that surrounds all of us. Some people may refer to that energy field as Akasha, and some may refer to it as the energy of light or source. Others may experience it as God. For me, it is less about what we call it and more about what we can do with it; how it impacts our soul's journey, our learning, and our essence.

This energy surrounds all of us and all of us can access it and do access it without awareness. It is the energy that suggests you contact a friend in need out of nowhere; it is the energy that guides your decisions – be it a call to a purpose, a love, a change of location or a change of heart.

It is that which guides us from deep within but it is not solely within. It is around; it is everywhere and it is nowhere. It is like the air. It is in my lungs and in the world, and in your lungs. It cannot be contained as one thing, and yet it is one thing: air. And that is you. You are like the air. You are nowhere and everywhere. You are in the physical, like the air comes into the lungs and is in the physical body, and you are non-physical, like the air surrounding you. And this paradox is the key to unlock your joy. It is in the knowing that we are both the physical manifestation of energy and, at the same time, the energy that surrounds us. There is then no beginning and no end to any one of us, or to anything.

This is my story. This is the story that was shared through me when I learned to connect to this energy field, as you can, as anyone can. This is my story into love, into my heart, into my true knowing of who I am. While I studied, wrote, blogged, podcasted, and taught on the true meaning of authenticity for a decade, I did not unlock the timeless nature and beauty of it until I understood the nature of our soul, our soul's journey, and the interconnected nature of all things.

I wish to take you on this journey with me, into the energy, the akasha, into the light that surrounds us and is us. I wish to take you with me on that journey so that you may too choose to unlock this field of light and join me and countless souls who have done the same. I am not a mystic and I am able to access this field of light. And so, it is my belief that the world will be a safer, happier, and a more joyous place if we can all unlock this energetic space for guidance into our potential. Most of us look to our achievements, to our relationships, to our mothers or fathers or even to a higher power source we hope surrounds us for answers. But our potential can be seen in an instant when we experience the light field that surrounds all of us.

And know it is available to all of us, and is us.

I wrote each lesson in this series to help me heal: heal my heartbreak, heal my unresolved emotions, even heal my life's melodramas. Each lesson led me one step further down my path because it was in the lessons that I moved deeper into my truth, into my authentic self, and towards my destiny. I learned we enter into divine motion, not when we achieve more, but when we unlock the next lesson in our soul's journey.

We are all able to experience ecstatic joy, and we are all the same in our desires to find love, meaning, and freedom: The freedom to be exactly who we are and where we are in every moment, despite the difficulties we may face. Because it is not in the overcoming of these difficulties that we truly experience joy, it is in the surrender that we find joy. It is in the surrender into the simplicity that we are already capable of endless love, endless joy, and endless happiness. We do not have to change, make more, do more, or be more. We can experience any state we desire, even when our surroundings suggest we should feel differently.

This is my story into the Akasha, into the light that is always ever-present. And this is a story into my heart, and the details of my journey with my soulmate. Yes, I found my soulmate in this life, and not just any soulmate, I found my twin flame. And

I, like a Hollywood movie, fell head over heels in love, as did she. And like a twin flame love can, we found that our love transcended logic, personal agendas, and just about any rationale that previously guided our decisions. We were in love and our love moved us to transform, to break down, to show up new and to decide ultimately if love would prevail.

And it was in this love that I found my way back to my truth - the truth that I am a writer. That I am a spiritual seeker. That I am on a path towards my destiny that I and only I hold the key to unlock my truth in this lifetime and lives to follow. And it was in love that I found the beauty, not of soulmate love, but of myself. And it was in love that I found that love of self was more important than any other love, any other motive, and any other agenda. As it seems that when you find love of your self, love of the person you choose to be in this lifetime, and you allow her to show up as she alone knows she is meant to, that all else fades into nothingness. It is not about fighting for your freedom to be in your truth with others, but it is about fighting for your freedom to show up to your self without hate, without fear, without arresting who you are for an idea of who you should be.

And it was in that love that I really understood how to let go. How to let love leave if it was not meant to be and flow when it is meant to. And if it is not given back, I still can give my love to myself. And if it is not taken care of, I can still love. And if I am harmed, I can always forgive, for it is in my nature to let the rivers of love continue to flow. And if I am sad or anxious or lost or lonely, I can always find my way back by knowing I am loved. I am love. We are all love. We are all made of the same fabric and just as we inhale and exhale until we take our last breath, we can allow the love within to flow just as easily.

So, I hope that you enjoy the lessons I learned and how I share them with you through the connection to the energy field of the Akasha. And more than that, I hope that you find the joy within, that you find the flow of love within you, and that you offer that love to yourself and to everyone surrounding you. And I hope that when and if that love is not reciprocated, you never stop loving yourself and others. And if you find you must walk away from love, never walk away from the love of your self. And finally, I hope you open your self to the light in whatever ways you can in all ways you can, and as often as you can.

With love,
Laura and the guided light energy of the Akasha.

the
nature
of
boundaries

Imagine your hands are tied

      behind your back with a rope.

Imagine the rope has large knots

      and is tightly bound around your wrists.

            You are seated on the floor,

helpless to solve the predicament you find yourself in.

Perhaps you are even tied to a pole,

in a basement,

in an unknown location

and the prospects of getting out

of this position are slowly

looking less and less promising.

You think to scream for help.

You think to pull your arms away

from the pole you are tethered to,

but you know none of these actions

will avail themselves towards a solution.

You sit in the quiet desperation that unfolds

as the reality settles in

that you may not have any way

to free yourself.

Without a realistic way to remove yourself

from this moment,

you begin to settle in;

you resign yourself to the reality

of your circumstances.

This moment,

    like other moments,

        unfolds in the only way it can

- in the present.

The panic of what the future may bring is

an obstacle to the mind because the reality,

the singular moment,

is simply what it is

- you,

tied to a pole, without any obvious recourse.

You return to the only thing that you have,

the present moment.

And in that moment,

You return to your breath.

You begin to watch your chest rise and fall.

You feel the weight of your body pressing into the floor.

You look up

and see the walls surrounding you

and the small window placed

above your line of vision.

And as you gaze out of the small window,

you begin to see the faintest visual

of the blue sky,

the fluffiest cloud,

and the tree that is blowing ever so slightly in the wind.

In the tree you see a bluebird.

The bird is seated on a branch.

Upon further investigation,

you see the bird's eyes staring out into the world,

much like your eyes are staring upon the bird.

The bird stands perfectly still

with no agenda,

with no purpose,

staring at the same blue sky and the same cloud.

You see the bird's freedom

– the bird can fly away at any moment

but his choice to sit and stare

at the same cloud and the same sky without movement.

As you gaze softly at this bird,

your body releases ever so slightly.

The tightness in your shoulders releases,

your chest settles back against the pole,

and your body settles into the floor beneath you.

While you are transfixed by the bird,

you hardly notice that with this release,

the rope that was previously bound so tightly,

that you saw no way to escape,

has released ever so slightly, too.

You move your left arm,

then your right arm,

and see that there is just enough space

to slip your hand from the rope.

And without struggle,

you slip your hand out with a single movement.

Your heart skips a beat with this sudden freedom.

You wiggle the other hand free

with little effort only to find

you are now seated on the floor,

arms free,

still transfixed on the bird in the window.

The bird has not moved its gaze,

nor have you moved yours.

You,   like the bird,

now have that freedom you so desperately desired

but find you no longer are grasping for its embrace.

You stand slowly.

You move towards the window,

crawl up through the opening and out,

and into the beautiful green field.

Moving carefully,

you keep your gaze on the bird

and the bird's gaze remains on the clouds in the sky.

Your newfound freedom feels less important

as you remain transfixed by the stillness of the bird.

You sit down in the field,

as you sat down on the floor previously,

and you stare at the sky,

at the bird,

and feel the breezes of spring blowing on your face.

You consider the fact that you could run,

be freer,

but you choose to sit exactly where you are

because you are exactly where you need to be

at all times.

No matter how dire the moment may seem to be,

you have exactly the freedom you desire

in every moment,

if you choose to see freedom as freedom in the mind.

And you have exactly what you need in all moments,

if you consider that all we ever need is within.

Just as the bird may choose to sit in the tree

even though he could fly away,

you may choose to sit still in life,

even when you could roam the endless fields,

fly over the mountains,

or sit by a pond in the sunlight.

You may be bound to a pole or

free in a patch of grass in the sunlight.

Either way you are free.

So when you find you are in a difficult situation

and you require the aid of another,

you can simply ask for the help you need.

You can ask

and see

if another wishes

to help you in your journey.

You may say, "I find myself in this most difficult

situation and require the aid of a friend or a lover.

I want that to be you. Would you happen to have a knife

I can use to remove the ropes around my wrists?"

But know true freedom is never freedom

from any one predicament.

You are already free.

Freedom is not in the removal of the ropes –

the removal of the predicament you face –

it is in the removal of the messages in the mind

that tell you removing the ropes is freedom.

A predicament is simply a moment in time

when you lack the resources you need to find a solution.

But you are not bound.

You are free.

You are always in the open air,

like the bird,

on the other side of an obstacle you may be facing.

But your life,

your path,

may be facing an obstacle

too big to handle alone.

Or the obstacle is unknown to you.

You may not have acquired the knowledge

of how to overcome what you face.

So, you ask for help.

And you receive what you need

to continue down your path,

into your joy,

into a full surrender to follow

in the footsteps paved towards your destiny.

And in the request for aid from another,

there are times when the other finds

they do not have the resources to help you.

They set a boundary.

They set this boundary

because they do not have the tools you require

to remove the ropes around your wrists.

Or, they may have the tools,

but do not have the desire to help you.

Or, they simply find they are bound in too many knots

of their own to offer a helping hand.

In these cases, smile peacefully.

Accept this boundary and request the aid of another.

Relax.

Breathe,

and notice that in the efforts to find the help you need
you begin to loosen the ropes
once felt so tightly around your wrists.

And when someone you love is tied to a pole
and you wish to help,
and you see how quickly you can release the ropes
with the knife you possess,

you must be careful.

Walk up slowly.

Offer your help with a gentle grace.

Begin with offering your assistance with love
and without fear of rejection.
"I happen to have the knife
you need to release those ropes."

But know that you may not be well received.

You may encounter a boundary.

Perhaps the ropes tied so tightly

around your friend or lover's wrists

have gone unnoticed.

They don't see they need the help

you see so clearly.

Perhaps the ropes are woven

into the fabric of their story

that life is a series of tight ropes

that must be removed without assistance.

They believe, "my life is one of my making

and these ropes are mine

and I must remove them myself."

When faced with this way of thinking,

you can only walk away,

knife in hand,

and not fight for their survival.

In no case can your help

do more than scare them into believing

you are the problem,

not the solution

to the predicament they face.

Your knife,

your assistance,

now becomes a threat.

So put your knife away and walk in peace.

Accept the boundary placed

because pushing your assistance onto them will result in

further injury,

as they will reject your offer

and see the knife as an attempt to harm them.

When someone sees a solution

as the problem,

know that they are

where they need to be

because they are learning

what they need to learn.

And perhaps what they need

to learn is how to fight

with the messages

of the mind that suggest

that life is a struggle

meant to be fought alone,

in a basement

without aid

from others,

filled with fear

and resistance to the truth.

The truth is that when love is present
in the form of a loving gesture,
it will help to at least fill the room with love.
And the presence of love
will always present more solutions than problems.

Because in the state of love,
we can see what we previously could not
– that we are guided, supported, and loved –
that we are love and in love we are free.

And when we know we are free
– we are not the problems we face,
but we are the love and essence behind the problems -
we accept the tools presented.

And if the tools are not helpful,

we accept the love offered.

Fear tells us to be mindful of the love offered

because the love could be masked as a threat to our survival.

We believe we must do everything alone

to avoid being hurt or disappointed

or, worse, betrayed.

And in that calculation,

we find we are alone to face life's problems.

Fear after fear sets us aside,

in a dark basement,

without the tools, or love or sun on our faces

to overcome what we cannot see.

So, we wish to be safe from those we believe can hurt us.

We wish to avoid the pain others inflict
when they are not able to offer love without fear.

Say you accept the love of another
and the love offered was not truly love
but love masked in fear.

Someone approaches you
with what feels like a desire to help,
but as you experience more and more assistance,
you begin to realize that this help is not
the help you need.

The knife you require is never in hand,

but a spoon,

a fork,

even a thermometer

is offered.

You begin to wonder,

"why is this fork being offered

when I am desperately in need of a knife?"

You see a shiny, sharpened knife

and begin to reach for just that,

but you are told you in fact need a fork.

And as you begin to wonder if,

in fact, you need a fork,

you see that a thermometer is now being suggested.

A thermometer?

You think.

Why would such a gift be replaced by what I require.

And you start to see that this person
would like to suggest you are not well,
and that you need their assistance
with not just cutting free from this moment,

but you require more.

And again,

you begin to wonder.

And in a moment, you see,

you only need a knife.

And you see that the agenda another possesses

is to not help you,

but to own you.

To control you.

To consume your time.

Your attention.

And bring you into a delusion that you are not well
and in need of constant assistance:
their assistance.

The help was not help
but a desire to control, own, betray,
or worse inflict harm upon you.

And while you may feel that their desires were about you,

they were the manifestation of their own fears.

In the desire to control, own, betray, or inflict harm,

they were simply acting from their own fears.

The fear of not belonging,

not connecting to themselves,

to others, to life,

and in this they need to control another:

you.

Was it a mistake to ask

and accept the love masked as fear?

Was there something you should have done differently

before asking for the help

that was not actually readily available?

Was there something you did to deserve

the helping hand that

turned into a lack of help

and a form of betrayal?

When someone offers help
and cannot succeed,
or worse causes additional harm,
simply turn back to the window.

Look at the bird.

Know that the bird is free to fly

but chooses not to,

and will face rain,

storms,

and even potentially losing the branch

he sits so gingerly upon.

And in that loss,

he simply flies up and   over to another branch

awaiting his arrival.

He may even face insurmountable obstacles

and overwhelming challenges

that leave him in the perils of life and death decisions.

And even with all that, he is free.

And even when life sends a blow,

and a betrayal of the worst kind,

he can begin to fly again with all his might

when he sees the betrayal

as another storm of life that blew through,

stole his branch,

but left him free to fly

quickly to the next branch in life.

It is in this awareness:

the rain is not here to beat him down,

but to help him fly.

The misguided aid of a friend

is not to be feared or meant to cause you harm,

and the world as we know it will not fall apart

if the help offered is not the help demanded.

We are only here to sing on a branch,

to fly with the winds,

and fight the storms with all our might,

until we cannot beat back death's door,

and then to try again.

It is in this that boundaries are set.

It is in this understanding that we are not alone:
that the help of others is as helpful as you accept it to be
and that the limits you place on your life
are as limiting as you want them to be.

And that your freedom,
the freedom to express fully,
stare out into the sun with the bird,
is always available to you,
if you let it be.

We can and only will be free,

truly free,

when we open our hearts

to the love we have within,

let others come in with the same love,

and set those free who,

after showing their constraints on love,

prove to be more trouble than worth

on our journeys towards our destinies

into our truest selves.

So, when help is offered freely,

accept it without hesitation.

And if the help offered doesn't seem to have value,
investigate any limitations you may have in your perception
that may lead you to reject the help you may need.

And when you need help

and assistance is not given,

accept the boundary placed,

the limits the other has on what they can offer.

Because any offering that is not given with love

will not avail towards a true solution.

.

Know that the limits placed,

the boundary placed,

is a limitation of actual resources

or a limitation in their minds

that suggests they are not enough,

able, or open to offering assistance.

And finally,

know that when you offer assistance to those unready,

you will not help, as much as you may try.

And

in that effort to help those unavailable to your offerings,

you can only harm yourself.

Offer with love.

And, walk away in love when your offer is rejected.

Smile.

Walk away with love in your heart
for you have offered love.

Anything rejected is never a rejection of you.

It is the rejection of love;

the rejection of the love they lack within.

Be free. Remain on your path.

Give without care of rejection

or another's acceptance of your offering.

And when stuck,

accept those gifts that aid you on your path in life,

and reject all that does not assist you.

Set a boundary

when the assistance is truly an obstacle on your path

and accept all boundaries placed,

even if you are confident that your assistance is of value.

Know this

and all friction amongst friends and lovers

will dissipate into the air like mist rising at daybreak,

off the field,

gently past the birds,

and into the limitless skies above.